RAILINGS

MARTYN TURNER

RAILINGS

Political cartoons

1998–2000

THE BLACKSTAFF PRESS BELFAST

Most of these cartoons, the wide screen ones, first appeared in the *Irish Times*. But those that are a different shape, sort of squarer, chances are they were commissioned by *The Scotsman, The Independent* (London) *or The Guardian,* bastions of the sterling broadsheet press.
My cartoons are distributed by The Cartoonists and Writers Syndicate, Riverside Drive, New York City.

In memory of Ernie Turner (1913–2000) and Mark Cohen (1945–1999), who spent their lives making the world a happier place for those who knew them.

First published in 2000 by
The Blackstaff Press Limited
Wildflower Way, Apollo Road, Belfast BT12 6TA,
Northern Ireland

© Text and cartoons, Martyn Turner, 2000
All rights reserved

Martyn Turner has asserted his right under
the Copyright, Designs and Patents Act 1988 to be identified
as the author of this work.

Printed by Guernsey Press Limited

A CIP catalogue record for this book
is available from the British Library

ISBN 0-85640-687-2

www.blackstaffpress.com

Introduction

In general, with these round-up-of-the-last-two-years-of-cartoons things, I put the cartoons in chronological order, bung in a few explanatory notes here and there and Bob's your uncle, or, to my reader in west Belfast, *is É Roibeard d'uncail* (I understand, from watching Sinn Féin MLA's on Channel 4, that no English is spoken there).

But the last two years have been extraordinary, in news terms, inasmuch as there have been only two major stories, north and south, dominating the headlines. In the south we have been painfully, slowly, uncovering the sleaze and corruption brought about by the de facto one-party rule of Fianna Fáil since the foundation of the state. We have discovered that we replaced corrupt undemocratic royal rule from Dublin Castle with corrupt undemocratic republican rule from the Dáil, from the banking system, the church and anyone else who was in 'the golden circle' and many other interlinked circles. Better to be screwed by your own, I suppose, than some foreign johnny . . . but not much.

In a state founded on resistance to authority, revolution (can you have right-wing revolutionaries?) quietly reaps the whirlwind down the years as loyal subjects brought up on tales of heroic resistance to authority rarely take rules, regulations and laws seriously. I'm not an enthusiast for rules myself but, as a Dubliner who willingly succumbed to six pages of regulations when he rented an apartment in Manhattan told me once, 'you sometimes realise that rules that are designed to make life more pleasant are a good idea'. The penny hasn't quite dropped down here. So good rules, like those covering littering, waste disposal, road safety, planning, non-resident foreign bank accounts, murder and suchlike continue to be ignored despite the occasional entreaties from the government, and we continue to live happily in our filth whilst waiting for that day when a twenty-year-old unlicensed, uninsured drunk driver comes at us on the wrong side of the road at ninety miles an hour and our widow/widower finds out if his/her insurance company is solvent.

No wonder surveys say that people are no longer interested in politics and current affairs. I sometimes feel the same way myself. The headlines are usually outside our field of daily frustrations. I get mad at the news, in a detached clinical way, every day. If I didn't I couldn't really do my job. But I get mad, really mad, I consider going back on a lifetime's opposition to capital punishment, every day when I think of the idiot who abolished milk bottles and the cretins who have made millions out of those awful, appalling, totally useless unopenable milk cartons we are now all forced to endure in our blessed republic. I would give my grade A number 1 vote to any party who promised to return the easily opened, recyclable, milk bottle to a fridge near me. Unless they had an armed wing, of course. Sorry, Gerry.

Speaking of which, the story in the north is similarly mono-thematic. How are they all coming to grips with the notion that some sort of democracy might be in the offing? Not very well, so far. All sides of the tribal divide seem to loathe the idea that they have to respect other people's strange ways or at least offer them tolerant indifference. One side (well part of one side) who only a few brief years ago were plotting to blow us to bits now lecture us on human rights. The other side can't even offer human rights towards their own fellow paramilitary brothers in arms and gaily do away with each other, and any of the vast army of neutrals who get in the way.

These sordid ways of life, and death, that pass for Irish civilisation on both sides of the border make the work of the satirist/cartoonist exceedingly difficult. How can you exaggerate the extreme? How could you invent some of the plots and sub-plots that are recounted to us on the front pages of the newspapers every day. Invent something crazy today and tomorrow you discover it actually happenened. Not that I am complaining; there are enough of my fellow sketchers in even more disgusting parts of the world locked up in chokey or currently residing in a graveyard that I can be grateful every day that, even though it is almost impossible to exaggerate the activities of what passes for politics in this 'ere neck of the woods, I am fully entitled, within the small leeway that our libel laws permit, to piss in the wind, figuratively, symbolically, every day. I'm thankful for that.

And to the viewer of my website who wrote to tell me that I look like the most miserable person in the world: don't worry, I'm constantly laughing, a little hysterically at times, of course.

Here endeth the lesson. Here beginneth the daft pictures. Happy Christmas, or Winter Solstice Fraternal Greetings to those of you who like to be politically correct.

MARTYN TURNER
KILDARE
SEPTEMBER 2000

Department of Foreign Affairs

It may be disingenuous to include Bill Clinton in this section as his affairs seemed mainly domestic but, nonetheless, here he resides. It could have been said of Clinton that at least, unlike many Americans, he made love not war. But residents of Iraq, where the population have been irradiated courtesy of good old American know-how and latterly Serbia, where America (and chums) used up most of their bombs lest they weren't 2YK compatible, know that Mr Clinton was able to do both at the same time.

His main chum, Mr Blair, was able to talk war at Serbia and at the same time talk peace in Northern Ireland. Northern Ireland resides firmly in foreign affairs as that is where it resides in the business of the Dublin government. Which is odd since, until a recent referendum, the Dublin government claimed Northern Ireland as part of its own.

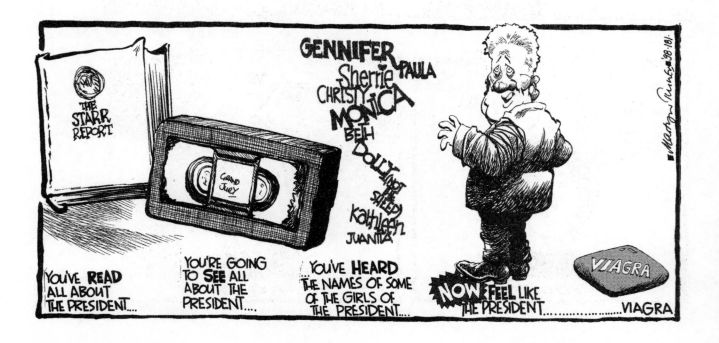

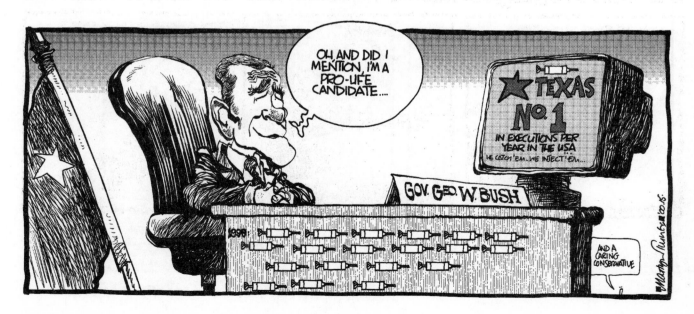

Chechnya

Putin and Chechnya

Tories and Friends

Into Africa

13

The Balkans

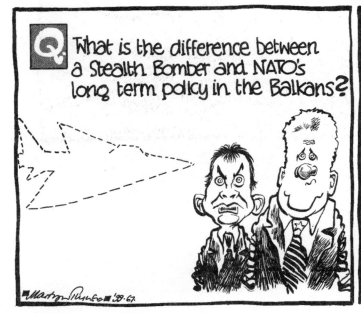

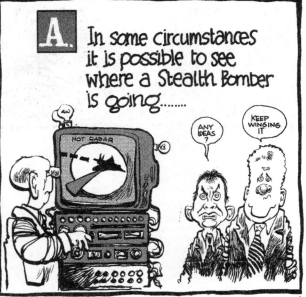

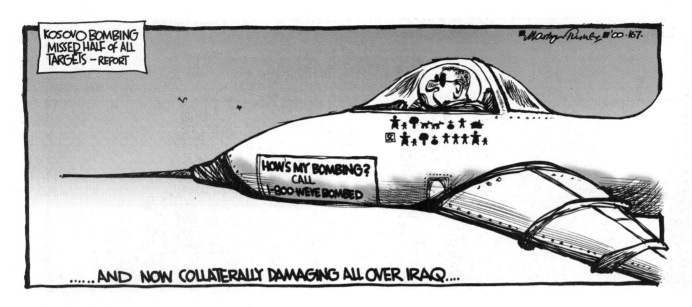

While Indonesia was actively slaughtering the population of East Timor they were invited to attend a British arms fair . . .

The North

MANSLAUGHTER

MAN'S LAUGHTER

The birth of Leo Blair coincides with the appearance of the N.I. Executive

30

32

Bob McCartney goes it alone . . .

THE SHAM FIGHT/SCARVA

THE SHAM APOLOGY/DRUMCREE

34

The *News of the World* launched a campaign to name and shame child abusers.

This section ends with a piece I wrote for the *Irish Times* after a five-week visit to Australia. Those who concur with the present Australian Prime Minister's view that policy towards the indigenous Australians is nothing to apologise for can dismiss the piece as propaganda since I should declare that part of my trip was organised by an Aboriginal rights group.

KOALAS next 1km.

EMU next 5km.

KANGAROOS next 500m.

IRISH CARTOONIST next 1metre

Beating about the bush

I think it was the third night in Australia, hereinafter known as Oz, that I woke and suspected I'd acclimatised. Oz is magical. I'd dreamt that I had invented an essential missing element for the Oz lifestyle – Breakfast Beer. I could make my fortune tapping in to this hitherto untapped market. I had them over a barrel. It was obvious. The only time of the day beer didn't seem readily available. A low alcohol, bright and cheery start to the day. I'd just pop round and talk to Tooheys, who seemed to be the big cheeses ale wise in Oz, and let them in on my big idea.

It's a stereotype, I was told. Australians are now falling down the beer consumption league table of the world way behind the Czechs, the Slovaks, the Latvians. How would you like it, they said, if Aussies went round saying all the Irish were drunken brawlers? 'That's interesting,' I said, 'we sit in the pub all day long arguing over the unfairness of that stereotype.'

But Colm's friend Phil, who was shepherding us around Oz, gave the game away. There used to be an immensely popular band in Sydney, he said (who were crap, musically speaking, he added) called Free Beer. They played badly to huge audiences for years under signs reading Free Beer Here Tonight (it was probably Tonite, if I know my showbiz). Well there you are. And with that we went down the Bottler, and bought another slab (that's twenty-four little bottles of beer wrapped in their own cardboard and cellophane).

When Captain Cook came upon Australia in 1770 the native population, numbering up to a million souls, with hundreds of languages, organised in 500 groups, hadn't got round to inventing alcohol. In the previous 50,000 years they had invented almost everything else necessary for a well-ordered functioning society; art, law, social order and boomerangs (which are used to get birds up in the air so that they can be caught for food). The introduction of alcohol has been a bit of a bummer for the Aborigines and a tiny minority of them have become some of the most inventively abusive drunks I have ever heard about.

A few days into the trip we left the group we were travelling with and went off to do cartoony things. Whilst I was in a resort hotel, an hour and a half by plane north of Sydney, giving away a prize at the Australian cartoonists' Oscars and showing slides ('101 Wacky Cartoons About Terrorism – An Introduction to Northern Ireland') they were going round schools and doing seminars and stuff. 'They' were, in the main, a mixed bunch of yoofs and their handlers from the Republic, Northern Ireland and Britain. One of the things they did was called 'Politics in The Pub', where they spoke about The Peace Process. The local Sydney cheerleaders for our former terrorists of the Republican persuasion were there, too, and proceeded to tell the throng about the horrors of being a Catholic Nationalist in Northern Ireland. The gentleman in question, it turned out, had never been to Northern Ireland. He came from Manhattan, bless him. One of our yoofs got up and pointed out that she was a Catholic, by tribe if not persuasion, from Ballymena and had never felt she was a second-class citizen. Another said, in responding to Mr Manhattan's view that maybe the war wasn't over yet, if it was all the same to Mr Manhattan, he would rather not shed his own blood in the interests of Mr Manhattan's politics.

If Mr Manhattan wants a spiffing example of oppression a little closer at hand he might take a quick glance at the history of the Aborigines, the native Australians. The policies, guns, diseases and laws of the British and European settlers reduced their population from an estimated million in 1770 down to around 200,000 in 1986. Since the native population wasn't included in the census in Australia until after 1967 (before that, I guess, they were part of the flora and fauna) it is hard to know exactly when and how this decline happened. The first Aborigines to be given voting rights were returned servicemen in 1949; this was extended in 1962 and then in dribs and drabs until they achieved full equal voting rights in 1987, that's, er, just twelve years ago.

*Whilst returned Aboriginal servicemen, in this land
that reveres the war dead above and beyond anything
you would see in Britain, were given the vote they
weren't allowed into Returned Servicemen's Clubs, the social
centres of Australia, for quite some time after the war.*

CORKS? NO,
MATE THAT'S
ANOTHER OF
THEM UNFAIR
STEREOTYPES..

Whilst the yoofs were in Sydney fighting for truth, justice and a
bit of common sense, we were observing the Floridisation of Australia.
This has nothing to do with putting chemicals in the water supply to
allegedly keep your teeth strong and healthy. It has to do with
inappropriate building practices. Oz is a magical place, it is as beautiful,
majestic, comfortable and attractive as any place me and Herself have
ever been. It has, sort of, indigenous building styles. They may involve tin
roofs but they are local tin roofs. What we saw in northern, coastal New
South Wales was American but not so chic. New just-built resort hotels (we
stayed in one, it was nice but it wasn't Australia) and, worst of all, behind
the lovely little town of Yamba, a development where they dig out channels
so every distinctive-slightly-different-but-really-all-the-same-bungalow
has its own piece of water to park the boat on. In other words,
Florida. We didn't see many Aborigines in these places. Actually I
don't think we saw any indigenous Aussies here at all.

*The pattern of population redistribution has left the Aborigines across the
mountains, away from the coast, into the interior, and in the north. Those left
in the cities tend to be ghettoised in places like Redfern in Sydney where they
can avail of all the opportunities social and racial discrimination has to offer.
See inner city areas in America, Britain, Ireland, for similar examples.*

*Maps are available showing that every square inch of Australia was
inhabited by one group or another before 1770. So wherever you are in Oz you
are standing on someone's native homeland. Sadly, in many parts of the East
coast there are no longer any natives left to support a home. Captain Cook
declared Oz to be a 'Terra Nullius' which meant, for those conversing in Latin,
that the land was empty and belonged to no one. Captain Cook must have
been optically challenged.*

*In the 1950s Britain detonated three atomic bombs in this supposedly empty
place, at empty places such as Emu, south Australia and Maralinga, SA.*

Aborigines inhabiting these empty places got radiation sickness.

In recent years court cases have slowly and painstakingly established the rights of the Aborigines to their own land. This is known as Native Title and is constantly under judicial and governmental review.

We spent three of our four weeks in Oz away from Sydney. Sydney is a magical place, too. The harbour is indescribable, so I won't bother. It is like all the photographs and films you have seen of the place times ten. Nothing prepares you for its size, beauty and grandeur. It fair dinkum takes your breath away, as they actually do say down under.

Back with the group we formed a convoy, minibus, minibus, air-conditioned four-wheel drive Pajero – the yoofs and us (I was in the air-conditioned four-wheel drive and nothing would budge me – old age has to have some compensations) and headed out of Sydney into the interior. Down the Parametta Road, past the Orange Order of New South Wales' Charity Shop, over the Blue Mountains, for three hours to go through a town called Orange. There is no getting away from Northern Ireland. Orange had an Orange Town Hall, an Orange golf course, Orange toilets and other Orange institutions and facilities. I forgot to look see if it had a Garvaghy Road where Orange men and women can parade all day long, blissfully, in the sunshine. (The week before we passed through Orange they had had hailstorms and floods, as had large areas of the interior. The week we left Australia five firefighters died in a bush fire in Victoria. Australia has big weather.) And then onwards for another seven hours, past rolling hills to the flat hot bush.

We spent a week or so staying in mainly Aboriginal towns and settlements; Weilmoringle, Brewarrina, the mining town of Lightning Ridge. We went to Gadooga, once voted the second most boring town in Oz where, on entering the local Bowling Club for lunch, we watched a fight break out on the adjacent cricket pitch. This didn't seem boring at all. We talked to Aborigines about their history, their

local sites and their culture, which these days can include Country Music Television off the satellite. We watched boomerangs and other stuff being made. Visited museums. Fished for yabbies in a muddy river and lost all sense of time and space in the vastness of the plains. We saw emus and kangaroos aplenty and slept under the stars (and I didn't snore, Herself is proposing I sleep outside back here in Kildare from now on). We visited the ruins of a mission.

Missions. It was decided somewhere, by someone, that Aborigines really ought to be just like white Australians. They should be assimilated. Civilised. To civilise them civilised society stole their children. Not very civilised. I'll repeat that, it takes a while to sink in. They stole their children. Government agencies, like dog catchers, travelled round picking up Aborigine children to place them with white familes or put them in church-controlled missions. There they did White Studies. English only spoken. What time to take afternoon tea. Cricket, how she is played. Christianity 101. That sort of thing, I expect. This programme helped to wipe out knowledge of local languages, history and customs. It created a whole bunch of people who don't know where they come from, who they are. Some remain to this day cut off from their families. They are known as the Stolen Generation. In the 1960s this policy was abandoned as after decades it still wasn't turning Aborigines into Australians and, maybe, because someone in government realised how totally horrendous it was.

These days the government talks of reconciliation. No one seems to be quite sure what this means. One theory is that it means the government want something sorted before the Sydney Olympics in 2000 so that the ongoing Aborigine Question might not be an embarrassment. I asked an Aborigine student what it was he wanted. 'It would be quite nice,' he said, 'if someone would say sorry. That would be a start.'

   Back from the bush we did other stuff. Oz is magical. We overviewed the farm where *Babe* was filmed. We saw blowholes and koalas, lunched at a place offering 'Battered Jews' on the menu ('The Department,' said the lady behind the counter, 'wants us to change the name of some of our fish.' Battered Blacks and Battered Whites were on the menu on other days). We tried to surf and the *Irish Times* almost lost a cartoonist in the riptide. We watched schools of children, all in their obligatory sun hats, being taught on the beach and thought that this must be the greatest place in the world to bring up children. We ferried around

Sydney, viewed the city from atop a revolving restaurant tower and from the *Sydney Morning Herald* offices (26th floor IBM Building. How do they work with a view like that?). Went to Canberra, which was a lot nicer than we expected, and did the slide show again in the Old Parliament Building. Outside the OPB limousines disgorged blushing brides for their wedding photos. Across the road are the wooden huts of the Aborigine Embassy, a protest site.

Oz is a delicate ecology. A while back they introduced European carp to clean greenery out of the channels in the cotton fields. After floods the European carp got into the river system, cleaned the rivers of all the green stuff that kept the rivers blue and sparkling and got rid of the native fish too. The rivers are brown and muddy now.

They introduced rabbits who are munching their way through the subcontinent as we speak.

They introduced cows and now they are introducing rape seed to feed the cows. The rape seed has gone native and is now taking over the bush, killing off the local plants. Spreading its yellowness all around.

They introduced foxes 'cos they wanted something to hunt.

They introduced, in 1770, a bunch of Europeans to a culture that had lived harmoniously with the earth for 50,000 years. Oz is magical. Aborigines have been disappearing ever since.

Department of Justice

Part of the European thing, that which made us rich beyond our wildest dreams, is to handle the stream of political migrants and asylum seekers that now do unto us what we have traditionally done unto the world at large – look for a better life abroad. To date, we have acted more like a bunch of Boston Irish who held out against bussing longer than any other part of the States, than the Ireland of the Welcomes we see in the Bord Fáilte ads.

I've stuck some of the tribunals stuff here, too, since its judges that oversee them. Relive again the moments when 'Will he fuck!' became legally part of the lingua franca as we learnt that our entire democracy was dependent upon the largesse of freedom-loving builders. Then there was the final uncovering of Mr Haughey's lifestyle and the associated shenanigans of bankers, businessmen and other people who considered it their sacred duty to make up their own rules as they went along.

50

The Tribunals

52

54

Mr Haughey's finances

It was alleged that some of the money intended for Brian Lenihan's liver tranplant went to finance the purchase of Mr Haughey's hand-made French shirts. Hard to believe.

58

The Banks

The Ansbacher Deposits

62

Frank Dunlop

James Gogarty

Department
of Agriculture

Same old, same old. I've always wondered why it is impossible to make money out of the one thing that we all need, food. But farmers manage it.

French farmers fed chickenshit to cows. Personally, he said smugly, I'm a vegetarian.

Department of Environment

P lease don't throw this book away. Recycle it. I shall do my best to recycle all the ideas in this book in future years. Well, I already have.

Department of Health

Someone estimated once, in England, that if smokers paid for the cost they incur to the health services, cigarettes would cost £12 each. Of course putting up the price of cigarettes (and drink) kick-started our inflation. So government policy is currently to try and keep down the price of addictive drugs.

Department of Finance

Isn't it great to have a Minister for Finance who is always right, even when he's wrong? And anyone who says he isn't right, is a left-wing pinko. It has always been my opinion that he is right, about as far right as you can get.

Department of Taoiseach

The main job of the Taoiseach these days is to distance himself from all the scandals and wrongdoings that go on around him. His greatest strength, he claimed in an interview, was his memory. What he meant to say was that his greatest strength was his *lack of* memory but he forgot to say that at the time. He forgets quite a lot, especially when he appears at the tribunals.

84

A year later . . .

90

91